THREE TALES OF
BASIL BRUSH

Peter Firmin

KAYE & WARD · LONDON

First published by
KAYE & WARD LTD,
21 New Street, London EC2M 4NT
as separate volumes
under the titles
Basil Brush and a Dragon, 1971
Basil Brush builds a House, 1973
Basil Brush Gets a Medal, 1973

First published in this edition under the title
Three Tales of Basil Brush Bumper '3 in 1' Book 2
1979

ISBN 0 7182 0332 1

Printed and bound in Great Britain by Cox & Wyman Ltd,
London, Fakenham and Reading

BASIL BRUSH AND A DRAGON

Basil Brush is a clever fox.
He likes to read stories to Harry the mole.

Harry has many story-books.
He has books about animals and birds.

He has exciting books about space-travel.

He has books about pirates and witches and dragons and other exciting things.

Each day Harry would choose
a different story.
"Today," he said to Basil,
"I will choose a story about a king;
a king who was bold, in days of old,
and killed a fierce bad dragon."

So Basil told Harry the story about
the king. It was about a fierce and fiery
dragon who frightened all the people.
The king put on his helmet and took
his lance. He rode on his brave horse
to kill the dragon.
Harry liked that story very much.

Basil and Harry went to bed.
Basil was tired and went to sleep.
Harry did not go to sleep at once.
"Basil," he said from his little bed.
Basil grunted.
"Basil," said Harry once again.
Basil snorted.
"May I ask you a question?" asked Harry.

"Tomorrow," grumbled Basil.
"May we go hunting for dragons?"
asked Harry.
"Tomorrow," mumbled Basil, as he dropped
off to sleep again.
Harry was pleased.

Next morning Harry was very busy.
He was busy in the tool-shed.

He was busy in the village.
He was preparing for a dragon-hunt.

Basil and Harry had their lunch.
"It will be exciting," said Harry.
"Just like days of old,
when kings were bold,
and went to hunt the dragon."
"What are you babbling about, old bean?"
asked Basil.
"We are going to hunt a dragon today,"
said Harry. "You said we could."

"Did I say that?" said Basil. "How silly! Well I don't think I can, not today."
"Surely you are not afraid?" said Harry.
Basil looked hurt.
"Of course I am not afraid," he said.
"If I had a lance I would hunt one. I'd be off like a shot, as you know."

"Well, come on, then," said Harry.
He took Basil to the tool-shed.
"Here is your lance," he said.
He gave Basil a long bean-pole.

"Oh dear, how kind," said Basil.
"It's just what I needed, a lance.
With this lance I'd be bold,
like those kings of old,
but I haven't a helmet like them."

Harry went into the tool-shed.
"Here you are," he said. "Here is your helmet. Try it on."
The helmet was a cardboard box.
Harry tied it on with string.
Basil looked out of a slit in the side.

"I feel quite bold," said Basil. "With a box on my head and a pole in my hand I could go to hunt a dragon. It's a pity that I have no horse."

Harry ran out of the garden.
Basil practised hunting dragons.

He swiped at the thistles.

He slashed at the grass.

He did feel quite bold.

"Your majesty," said Harry.
"The royal horse is ready."
Harry led Basil to the garden gate.

"That's a very odd looking horse,"
said Basil. "More like a dish-mop on legs.
Are you sure that it isn't a dog?"

"Well yes, this is Alfred," said Harry.
"He is very good at hunting rabbits.
He probably hunts dragons too.
Shall we go?"

So the king rode out from his castle
on his brave horse.
His faithful servant ran on ahead
to find a dragon.

They stopped at the top of a hill.
"Look," said Harry. "Far across the meadow
I see a fierce dragon, I see its shape
against the sky."
"Forward! brave Alfred," called Basil.
"Forward to hunt the dragon!"
Alfred did not move.
"I think you say 'Rabbits'," said Harry.

"Rabbits!" cried Basil.
The brave horse wagged its tail, and ran.
The king rode over the meadow
to hunt the fierce dragon.

His brave horse carried him almost into the dragon's mouth. He plunged his lance deep into the dragon and fell off.

Alfred dug into the earth around the dragon's feet. The dragon fell to the ground.

"Oh, your majesty!" said Harry.

"That was well done. It was brave and exciting and bold."

"It was nothing," said Basil.
"That dragon was not very fierce.
Let us go and find another."

The king sat on his brave horse.
His faithful servant looked around.
"Look!" said Harry: "Beyond the wood,
behind the trees, I see a dragon moving."

"Forward! brave Alfred," Basil called.
"Forward to hunt the dragon!"
Alfred stood still.
"Don't forget to say 'Rabbits'," said Harry.
"Rabbits!" called Basil.

The king rode into the wood.
He rode through the trees to hunt
the fiery dragon.
The dragon stood on a wall
stamping its six legs in anger.
"Over, brave Alfred," cried Basil.

Alfred ran right up to the wall and then stopped. The king did not stop. He flew over the wall and plunged his lance into the dragon.

The dragon fell in a heap around the king and was still.

It was not fiery. It was wet.

From a house nearby came a shout.
"Is it a maiden in distress?" asked Harry.
"No, old chap," said Basil.
"It is a housewife in the kitchen.
Let us go somewhere else to find
a dragon."

The king rode back through the trees.
He rode up to the top of the hill.
His faithful servant looked around
but he did not see any dragons.
"I think the dragons have gone to sleep,"
said Harry. "It is getting late."

"Yes you are right," said Basil.
"See, my brave horse is thirsty.
His tongue is hanging out."
"Look," said Harry. "Your castle is near.
I will go and prepare a feast."

So the king rode back to his castle.
His faithful servant went ahead
to prepare a feast.

The king and his servant had their feast in the castle. They had soup and beans, and there were biscuits for the horse.

"Alfred must go now," said Harry. "It is getting dark. His master will be coming home from work."

"Goodbye, Alfred," said Basil. "I hope you will come hunting again."

Alfred wagged his tail as Harry took him to the door.

"Listen!" said Harry. "I hear a strange noise. I hear a grinding and a rumbling and a roaring. Can it be a dragon?"

Basil took up his lance. They all went outside to look for the dragon.

"There it goes!" said Harry.

The eyes of the dragon glowed in the dark.

Its dark shape lumbered over the field.
"Let us follow this dragon," said Basil.
"It is a very large dragon, so we will
wait until it goes to sleep."

The dragon stopped. It shut its eyes.
Alfred barked and ran towards it.
"Forward!" shouted Basil.

They ran shouting towards the sleeping dragon. They did not reach the dragon. They bumped into something else.

It was the farmer, returning from the field where he had left his combine.
"Hullo!" he said. "What are you three up to?"
"We were going to fight the dragon," said Basil. "That wild dragon over there."

"That's no wild dragon," laughed the farmer. "That one is tame, and it works for me. It helps me to gather the harvest. The only dragons I know are in the story-books, and that's the best place for them, if you ask me!"

Harry the mole has many story-books.
His favourite one is about a dragon.
"Look," he says. "There's a dragon in this story-book. And that's the best place for it if you ask me!"
Then he closes the book with a bang.

the end

BASIL BRUSH BUILDS A HOUSE

Basil Brush is a friendly fox.
He lives in a house in the country.

Basil has many friends,
but they don't all live in houses.

Arthur the dog lives in a barrel.

The coots live in a nest on the lake.

The doves live in a dove-cote.

And the bees live in a hive.

There are many different kinds of houses.
And Harry the mole lives in a hole.

One morning Basil went to see Harry.
"Good morning!" he called down the hole.

Harry came out of the door looking very wet and rather cross.
He carried a mop.
"What a night!" he grumbled. "It rained and it rained and the rain came in my roof."

"Did you get wet?" asked Basil.
"Wet!" moaned Harry. "My sitting-room is soaking and my dining-room is damp. The walls are all wet and so am I!"
"Well, why live in a hole in the ground?" asked Basil. "Why not live in a house?"
"Whoever heard of a mole in a house?" said Harry. "A mole always lives in a hole."

"Try something different," said Basil. "Don't be an old stick-in-the-mud. I know a dry place and I'm sure that it's free. Come and see."

Basil took Harry to the farmyard.
He showed him Arthur's barrel.

"Now, here's a fine house," said Basil.
"A barrel won't let in the rain.
The farmer is away and he has taken his dog.
Why not try it for a while?"

So Harry moved into the barrel.

"Good morning!" said Basil, next morning.
Harry poked his nose out of the barrel.
He looked cross and rather tired.
"What a night!" he grumbled. "I did not sleep a wink."
"Why," said Basil. "What kept you awake?"

"It was so noisy," said Harry. "There were cows mooing and pigs grunting and as soon as the sun rose, the cock began to crow. This house is too noisy for me."

"Well, try something different," said Basil. "I know of a place that's just right. It's quiet at night and I know that it's free. Come and see."

Basil took Harry into his garden.
He showed him the greenhouse.
"Now, here's a fine house," said Basil.
No cows or pigs to wake you in the night.'

"And in the morning?" asked Harry.
"You can sleep late," said Basil. "In fact I'll bring you breakfast in bed, old chap!"

So Harry moved into the greenhouse.

"Good morning!" said Basil, next morning, as he opened the greenhouse door.

"I thought you would never come," gasped Harry.

He looked cross and rather hot.

"Better late than never," laughed Basil.

"I've brought you some tea and toast."

"Toast!" exclaimed Harry. "With the sun beating down, this place is like an oven. I feel I've been toasted myself! Your greenhouse is too hot for me."

"Why not try something different?" said Basil. "I know of a place that's just right. It's cool all day long and I know that it's free. Come and see."

Basil took Harry down to the lake.
He showed him the nest of a coot.

"Now, what about this?" asked Basil. "It's soft and very dry. It's sheltered from the rain and the breeze in the morning is cool."

So Harry moved into the coot's nest.

That night it rained again.
Harry was cool and he did not get wet.
There was a big leaf over his bed
to keep out the rain. But the lake filled
up and the coot's nest floated out into
the middle of the water.

"Good morning!" called Basil, next morning. "Are you having a sail on the lake?"

"A sail!" shouted Harry. "I don't like sailing. I want to come ashore."

The cool morning breeze blew on the big leaf. The nest sailed across to the other side of the lake.

Basil ran round and helped Harry ashore.

"You were kind to help me," said Harry.
"But I do think a house should stay
where it is put.
I would like a house that is fixed."
"Let us try something different," said
Basil. "I remember a place that will do.
It is fixed to a post and I know that it's
free. Come and see."

Basil took Harry to the orchard.
He showed him the dove-cote.
"Do you fancy this house?" said Basil.
"I'll help you move in if you like.
It stands on a post. You see, it won't move. And the doves have flown away, long ago."

"It is lovely for doves," said Harry. "They can fly in and out of the windows. But it has no ladder and you know I can't fly. That house is too high for me."

"Oh, you are an old fusspot!" said Basil. "But there is just one more place I know. It's quite near the ground and I think it is free. Come and see."

Basil took Harry to the flower garden.
He showed him the bee-hive.
"Now that is more like a house," said Harry. "I think that will make a good home."

So Harry moved into the bee-hive.
"Good morning!" said Basil, next morning.
"You're up early today. Did you sleep well
Harry was sitting in the flower bed.
"Oh, I slept well enough," he answered.
"But the bees have come back and
they don't want me there.
That house is too crowded for me."

"What a shame," said Basil, "but never you mind. You can't share a house with the bees. Now I know the sort of house that you want, I'll build you a house of your own."

Basil took wood and bricks
and blocks of stone.
He built a house for Harry.

It was dry.
It was quiet.
It was cool.
It was fixed.
It was comfortably close to the ground.

"My very own house!" said Harry.
"I'll soon make it into a home."
"I'll leave you to move in," said Basil.
"House-building is tiring. I'm going to bed.
I'll see you in the morning."

Next morning Harry was first up.
He banged on Basil's door.

"Come and see what I have done," said Harry. "That house that you built was ideal, and I've made it into a home for a mole. It's just right for me. Come and see."

"What have you done?" said Basil.
"You have covered it over with earth.
I built you a house that was fit for a mole.
Now it is only a hole in the ground!"

"That's right," said Harry. "It's perfect. Now it's just the right home for a mole. I could never live happily in a house. A mole always lives in a hole!"

THE END

BASIL BRUSH GETS A MEDAL

Basil Brush is a helpful fox.
He tries to help others whenever he can.

He helps old people.

He helps children.

He helps animals and birds.
Basil Brush got a medal
for being so helpful.

Harry is a mole.
He tries to be helpful too.

Basil and Harry went to a palace.
In the palace lived a princess who had a big box of medals.

She liked to give medals to people who had done something very special.

There were other people waiting outside the palace gates.
There was a very brave soldier.
There was a clever inventor.

There was an actress who had acted for years on the stage and a nurse who had saved many lives.

They had all come to get medals from the princess, and Basil had come for a medal, too, for being such a helpful fox.

"I've come for my medal," said Basil to the gate-keeper. "Will you open the gate with your key?"
"We've come for ours too," said all the other people. "Why are we waiting so long?"

"I would open the gate if I could," said the gate-keeper, "but I cannot open it yet."

"If you've lost your key," said Harry the mole, "I've something here that might do. It's a nail that I picked up on the road. Could you open the gate with a nail?"

"Oh, I have the key," said the gate-keeper, "but the gate must stay shut till the princess is ready. She always has breakfast before she gives medals, and she has no fresh milk for her porridge.
When the farmer brings milk for the royal porridge, then I may open the gate."

Basil and Harry went to the farm.
They went to see the farmer.

"The princess needs milk for her porridge," said Basil. "Will you send milk to the palace?"

"I would send milk for the royal porridge," said the farmer. "The milkmaids are waiting to milk the cows. But the cows have not come from the meadow."

Basil and Harry went up to the meadow.
They went to see the cowman.

"The milkmaids are waiting," Basil called.
"They are waiting to milk the cows.
The farmer needs milk
to take to the princess.
She has no fresh milk for her porridge.
Will you bring the cows to the farm?"

"I would bring the cows to the farm," said the cowman, "but the bridge is broken and the cows cannot cross."

"If the bridge is broken," said Harry the mole, "I have something here that might do. It's a nail that I picked up on the road. Could you mend the bridge with a nail?"

"We need more than a nail," the cowman said.
"We need wood to mend the bridge.
If you go to the forest and ask the woodman,
he will cut down a tree."

Basil and Harry went to the forest.
They went to see the woodman.

"The bridge is broken," Basil said.
"Will you please cut down a tree?
We need some wood to mend the bridge
for the cows to cross over
to go to the farm
to give fresh milk for the princess.
She has no milk for her porridge."

"I would cut down a tree,"
the woodman said, "but my axe is blunt
and my grindstone is dry."

"If your axe is blunt," said Harry the mole,
"I have something here that might do.
It's a nail that I picked up on the road.
Could you sharpen your axe with a nail?"

"A nail will not do," the woodman said.
"I need water for the grindstone.
I sent my wife to the well for water,
but she has not come back yet."

Basil and Harry went to the well.
They found the woodman's wife.

"Where is the water?" Basil said.
"Your husband needs water
to wet the grindstone to sharpen his axe,
to cut down a tree to mend the bridge.
The bridge must be mended
for the cows to cross over
to go to the farm
to give fresh milk for the princess.
She has no milk for her porridge."

"I would bring water," said the woodman's wife, "but the handle is broken. The well will not work!"

"If the handle is broken," said Harry the mole,
"I have something here that might do.
It's a nail that I picked up on the road.
Could you mend the well handle with a nail?"

"That nail *will* do," said Basil Brush. "A nail is just the thing to mend the handle of the well."

So the handle was mended.

The woodman had water.

The axe was sharpened.

The tree was cut down.

The bridge was mended.

The cows crossed over.

The milkmaids milked the cows.

The fresh milk was taken to the palace, and the princess had milk for her porridge.

"Now I may open the gate," said the gate-keeper, "and the princess will give you your medals."
So he opened the gate, the people went in, and the princess gave them all medals.

One for the soldier.

One for the inventor.

One for the actress and one for the nurse.

Basil Brush got a medal
for being so helpful.

Only Harry did not get a medal.

"Because you are such a special mole,"
said the princess,
"I will give you a special gift."
She gave Harry a silver bowl and a spoon.
"It's a gift for a helpful mole," she said.
"I do like fresh milk with my porridge."

THE END